PLATFORM PAPERS

QUARTERLY ESSAYS ON THE PERFORMING ARTS
FROM CURRENCY HOUSE

No. 45
November 2015

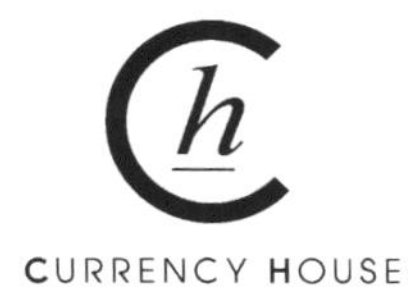

Platform Papers Partners

We acknowledge with gratitude our Partners in continuing support of Platform Papers and its mission to widen understanding of performing arts practice and encourage change when it is needed:

Gillian Appleton
Neil Armfield, AO
Anita Luca Belgiorno Nettis Foundation
Jane Bridge
Katharine Brisbane, AM
Elizabeth Butcher, AM
Penny Chapman
Robert Connolly
Peter Cooke, OAM
Rowena Cowley and Dr Richard Letts, AM
Michael J. Crouch, AO
Ian Enright
Larry Galbraith
Tony Grierson
Gail Hambly
Wayne Harrison, AM
Campbell Hudson
Professors Bruce King and Denise Bradley, AC
Peter Lee
Roderick H. McGeoch, AO
David Marr
Harold Mitchell, AC, AO
Joanna Murray-Smith
Helen O'Neil
Martin Portus
Lesley Power
Professor William Purcell
Geoffrey Rush, AC
Dr Merilyn Sleigh
Positive Solutions
Seaborn Broughton Walford Foundation
Sky Foundation
Maisy Stapleton
Augusta Supple
Andrew Upton
Rachel Ward, AM and Bryan Brown, AM
Kim Williams, AM
Professor Di Yerbury, AM

To them and to all subscribers and Friends of Currency House we extend our grateful thanks.

Platform Papers Readers' Forum

Readers' responses to our essays will from now on be posted on our website.

Currency House invites readers to send us considered responses to this or previous Platform Papers in length between 250 and 2000 words. Submissions may be emailed to info@currencyhouse.org.au with a brief biographical note. The Editor welcomes opinion and criticism in the interest of healthy debate but reserves the right to monitor where necessary.

Platform Papers, quarterly essays on the performing arts, are published every February, May, August and November and are available through bookshops, by subscription and on line in paper or electronic version. For details see our website at www.currencyhouse.org.au.

PAYING THE PIPER: There Has to be a Better Way

CATHY HUNT

ACKNOWLEDGEMENTS

I would like to thank the small-to-medium arts organisations with which I have worked over the years and acknowledge the time that so many of their members spent in good faith preparing expressions of interest in receiving six-year funding from the Australia Council, only for that program to be suspended. I would also like to acknowledge federal and state government staff in those bureaucracies (including the Australia Council Board and staff) who are our frontline in dealing with the whims of governments; and in particular those individuals behind ArtsPeak and #freethearts who ensured the voices of the small-to-medium sector would be heard. Among them Nicole Beyer, Norm Horton, Sarah Moynihan and Tamara Winikoff.

Particular thanks are due to those individuals from Queensland arts organisations whom I consulted; my co-author for Platform Paper No.15, Phyllida Shaw; the authors of previous Platform Papers I have cited; Professors Julianne Schultz and Justin O'Connor whose work I have drawn upon; Belinda Drew and Peter Shergold for their guidance on the growth of impact investing over the last three years; and the readers of the first draft of this paper, David Fishel, Mark Fenton, and especially Leigh Tabrett for the thinking and editing she contributed. Finally, of course, I once again thank Currency House editor Katharine Brisbane for her support, editorial assistance and desire for this dialogue and debate.

About the Author

Cathy Hunt is a cultural strategist based in Brisbane and one of the founding Directors of Positive Solutions, a consultancy specialising in the cultural and non-profit sectors. She grew up in the UK and her work in the arts there included being founding director of the Liverpool Festival of Comedy. Having initially studied literature and theatre, she also undertook, through the School of Architecture at Liverpool University, an MPhil on the design and development of buildings for the performing arts. As a consultant her focus has been on funding and financing; working with governments on arts and cultural policy; with organisations and artists on business planning and capacity building; and with communities on the development of new facilities for the arts. Among these were the Godinymayin Ijard Rivers Arts and Culture Centre in Katherine and the early plans for the West Kowloon Cultural District in Hong Kong.

Cathy is one of the founders of the QuickstART microloan fund for artists, now managed by Foresters Community Finance; and a consortium partner in the Queensland Arts Business Innovation Fund (ABIF). Following her involvement in Prime Minister Kevin Rudd's 2020 Summit, she became engaged in the *New Models New Money* research initiative driven by the Centre for Social Impact Studies (UNSW) and Arts Queensland.

As well as her 2008 Platform Paper *A Sustainable Arts Sector: What will it take*? she has written on cultural policy and financing the arts for the *Griffith Review.*

As a director of the non-profit company *Of One Mind,* Cathy is working with the Southbank Centre, London, to develop the Women of the World (WOW) Festivals in Australia and the Asia-Pacific. She was one of the executive producers of WOW Brisbane in June 2015.

Foreword

They say a week can be a long time in politics. In the week this paper goes to press Malcolm Turnbull has been elected Prime Minister of Australia and announced the appointment of Senator Mitch Fifield as Minister for Communication and the Arts. In the immediate future, the arts sector waits to see if the new leadership will overturn the decision by predecessor Minister George Brandis to redirect more than $120 million from the Australia Council budget, to Ministerial control. This question has its own far-reaching resonances. But this paper argues that the Brandis decisions demonstrate the extreme fragility in national arts funding arrangements, and that, if the Federal Government really believes that the arts can play a role in the 'innovation' agenda of the future, it needs to demonstrate innovation in its own approach to funding and financing the long-term health and stability of those individual artists and organisations that make up the sector.

Underlying the Brandis decision is the idea that providing grants 'for excellence' will produce more of it. In fact, excellence takes time, investment, and opportunities for experimentation to achieve. There is no point in considering the notion of excellence unless there are strong, confident and ambitious artists and organisations to take risks and develop their work to a standard of which they and their community can be proud. This needs to be the starting point for the future.

1. Introduction

It was seven years ago in 2008, just before the election of Kevin Rudd, when I wrote a Platform Paper with my observations on sustainable models for the arts sector in Australia.[1] The commission for this second paper, exploring again the issue of funding and financing the arts, came as a result of the drastic cuts in public spending, including in the arts, in Queensland by the Newman Liberal National Party (LNP) Government in 2013. We chose to wait for 18 months to observe the impact but before I could begin it was eclipsed by a significant event in the national arts funding arena. In the May 2015 budget, the then federal Arts Minister, George Brandis, announced that $123.3 million would be removed from the Australia Council budget allocation over four years, of which a proportion would be placed at the disposal of the Minister himself for the purpose of creating a new National Program for Excellence in the Arts.[2] The news galvanised the arts community and social media like nothing since the Australia Council was first mooted. A Senate Inquiry into Commonwealth Arts Funding is sitting and has received a record number of submissions from individuals and organisations in all states and territories.

Since the publication of that first paper (co-written with UK colleague Phyllida Shaw) I have been working on a series of research projects and the implementation of new funding schemes to introduce more money into the sector—beyond program grants (whether from governments or philanthropists)—and to increase support towards more sustainable modes of operating for artists and arts organisations. The experience I have had in that time, coupled with this recent disregard of considered and professional funding processes at both state and national levels, has confirmed my view that we have reached the 'use-by-date' of a funding system that has served the sector adequately for the past forty years but is no longer fit for the purpose.

In fact (as Leigh Tabrett concluded in Platform Paper 34),[3] there never has been a coherent national system for funding and financing the arts in Australia. We have a group of agencies at different levels of government (as well as more and more foundations and individuals) that may be interactive and interdependent but certainly do not form an integrated whole and can still make unilateral changes without regard to their impact on the other players. Call it what you like, but it is not what we need to build a 'culturally ambitious nation'.[4]

The Federal Government funding decisions have impacted on the funding decisions and frameworks for all states and territories and will have flow-on effects for the plans of philanthropic foundations and sponsors engaged with the arts. The relationships within the sector itself have been fractured once again between the haves and the have nots—all fearful of losing the crumbs that fall from the table. As artistic director of Opera Queensland, Lindy Hume said in her recent *Artshub* article, *'the ideal of a creative flow connecting all sectors in the Australian arts community is under threat'.*[5]

The opportunity to create a stable national infrastructure of six-year funded organisations, proposed by the Australia Council for the first time in 2014, has been lost, as have thousands of hours invested by the 400-plus organisations which prepared expressions of interest in response to the Council's invitation. And perhaps the biggest loss of all is that the decision will reverberate on those bringing to the stage, or the walls, or the Kindle, or the big screen, contemporary Australian stories, new voices of the nation, new ways of innovating in the art form; and on the first step in the ladder for graduates in the arts and creative industries. Is this really the way to treat a nation's culture and the research bed of a multi-million dollar industry?

Although this is not the first time (nor will it be the last) where such petty decisions and paltry amounts of money impact on the short to medium term development of the arts, it is at a crucial time and could be just the beginning. At the time of writing the UK Government has requested that the Department of Culture Media and Sport (DCMS) prepare plans for either a 25% or 40% cut in public expenditure by 2019/20,[6] the kind of move that often portends change in Australia. But unlike the UK, we don't have the National Lottery to fall back on. Arts Council England (ACE) has built up £325 million in lottery reserves over the past five years, and it is now accepted practice that ACE can use both its government grant and proceeds from the Lottery Fund for the core funding of the national portfolio of organisations (the equivalent of our majors and key organisations).

If we think everything may change for the better with an election in 18 months time then we should think again. How long did it take to form a National Cultural Policy under the last Labor Government and what money was left in that Government at the end of the day to implement its recommendations? And it wasn't former Treasurer Hockey who wrote the following in the *Financial Review* earlier this year but Shadow Treasurer Chris Bowen:

> *Tough decisions will be necessary. The days of big spending programs will be over. The whole gamut of savings and revenue measures needs to be on the table.*[7]

We are living in a different world post the 2008 financial crisis and the prolonged period of weak economic performance that is being experienced by all Western nations. This is not helped in Australia by the failure (as yet) to find an appropriate taxation system to generate the income necessary to deliver the services required for a growing and aging population.

Developments in technology and the breakdown of trade, travel and communications barriers between countries and continents, are shaping a new world order in which the structures within and relationships between public, private and independent (non-profit) sectors are changing. There are new forms of corporate entity (the growth of B Corporations globally and Community Interest Companies in the UK);[8] increased activity in mergers and alliances across all sectors (including non-profit); new thinking about roles within government (responsibilities of Ministers, public servants and government-owned entities); and new approaches to funding and financing including the growth of impact investing.[9] You can even get a McDonalds without a box!

Even before the recent announcement, I was concerned that while the arts sector has been focused on trying to prove to governments that there is real public value generated by the arts and it is value worth paying for, governments were already busy seeking new ways and new partners to pay for that value across all the traditional services for which they have had responsibility, including education, health and social services. Our language and our arguments for increased funding have been formed around a particular way of working which is rapidly changing around us. The actions of the Queensland Government in 2013 and subsequently Minister Brandis as Arts Minister in the Federal Government in 2015, have not only accelerated the need for this discussion but demonstrate the damage that can be done if stakeholders don't work together to assist artists and arts organisations through this tumultuous time.

So I shall go back to some of the ideas that we put forward in the 2008 paper, and look at where we have made progress and where there are still significant hurdles to overcome. I'm going to look at what the impacts have been in Queensland and what could be the implications from the recent Federal Government decisions depending on the findings from the Senate Inquiry and the decisions of the new Arts Minister. Incorporating some of the ideas from recent Platform Papers and conversations with other respected colleagues, I will propose some of the changes we really need; why now more than at any other time in the history of arts and cultural development in Australia; and how we ensure once and for all, that whoever pays the piper in the future, it is the piper who calls the tune.

2. The age of some certainty

It was 2008 when my colleague and I set out to write Platform Paper No.15 (pre the global financial crisis and at the start of another mining boom) and we wrote it in response to the growing trend by governments (of both parties and at all levels) to demand more 'viable' or 'sustainable' arts organisations. We were seeing Ministers who didn't understand why organisations should attract continuous government support year in year out. They were unprepared to increase their arts budgets to cope with new players in the sector and wanted to free up existing resources to fund new demand and new work.

There seemed to be misunderstandings and poor communication (on both sides) about why arts organisations existed; why governments funded them and the business models that governments at all levels had helped to create and uphold and under which the sector had operated for decades. We wanted to unpick what the real debate was about; to challenge the language and articulate what the characteristics would be of a) individual organisations and b) the sector, if both were to survive (if not thrive) into the future. We expressed this at the time as 'sustainability', meaning the capacity to survive over the long term. Some of the characteristics have since been developed further by others in the context of resilience theory,[10] and understanding of intangible assets—those of social and cultural value which help build organisational and financial resilience.

We defined what the characteristics of a more 'sustainable' arts organisation and sector would be and what might need to change to achieve this. For example we suggested that a sustainable arts organisation would demonstrate:

- *a vision and purpose that are supported by its board, staff and funders*
- *confidence in its purpose and its plans, and its core products reflecting and promoting that vision*
- *regular renewal of its products through listening and learning from the consumers*
- *clear communication within and beyond the organisation and public support for its aims*
- *a diverse financial base, balancing earned and contributed income.*

And for the sector, it needed:

- *a balance of diverse and strong organisations of every scale and in all areas of the arts*
- *good communication and interaction between different parts of the sector*
- *individuals with skills, training and confidence, and with clear career pathways through the sector*
- *a healthy ecology at all levels, starting with early education, including opportunities for participation and professional practice, and encompassing community, government-funded and commercial sectors*

- *the support of a diverse range of communities and multiple ways in which individuals can engage with it.*

The paper looked at the UK and Australian situations at the time—the programs that had been put in place during the previous 15 years to strengthen the sector in the UK (all with their wonderful names Survive, Sustain, Thrive etc.) and the 'reviews' that had been the feature of the Australian landscape during the Howard Government including the Major Performing Arts Inquiry (Nugent) reporting to Government in 1999. We also wrote about a range of positive government (usually state) or sector-driven initiatives in Australia, which had strengthened the ecology of the sector as a whole: across subsidised and commercial operations; across supply and demand; and across art form and creative practice. Here was a range of initiatives that were working to create change for the better, in terms of the art created, the communities engaged, and value for money from the 'public purse'.

We recommended some things that have subsequently been taken on board by funding agencies, including government support to artists and organisations for the quality of their work and the value they create, regardless of their legal and operating structures; increased support of mid-career artists; and one of the most crucial, the move to longer-term funding arrangements for all organisations, not just those included in 1999 within the Major Performing Arts classification.

We also raised four key issues, which I believe have still not been addressed and which, considered together with our rapidly changing and destabilising external environment, have led us to the dilemma we have today. They are:

- the continuing poor understanding in some parts of government of the ecology of the sector;
- the limited sources of funding and financing that are in place for the arts at a 'system' level as well as the lack of diversity of income sources for individual artists and arts organisations;
- the responsibility for the gathering and dissemination of knowledge and information and for the sector's advocacy; and finally,
- the need for new approaches to the development of the sector into the future.

3. A short but relevant detour

Before considering each of these in turn it is worth looking at the impact of the 2013 funding cuts to the arts in Queensland. It is relevant because of how it happened, what has come about as a result, and because it sets a context (the impacts have already been felt) and tests some of those characteristics of sustainability we articulated back then.

I'd been through political change many times and seen the impact for the arts under governments driven by extremes of ideology including Thatcher's Britain and far-left Militant-run Liverpool City Council.[11] I was aware of the history of Queensland politics—and that is what I thought it was—history. In moving to Australia permanently in 1997 we had as a family chosen to live in Queensland. It was a time of great change. In Brisbane there was a purposeful re-focusing of the city on its greatest natural asset, the river, and the start of serious engagement with our Asian neighbours. We were part of the changing cultural landscape, undertaking the very first feasibility and business plan for the conversion of the Brisbane Powerhouse into a cultural centre; undertaking cultural planning for many local governments;

and engaging with the growth of Indigenous art centres across the Cape and Torres Strait. I had great respect for Joan Sheldon, Arts Minister and subsequently Chair of a number of arts organisations;[12] as well as for the immense changes brought about under the leadership of Anna Bligh as Premier and Arts Minister. Then suddenly, with the election of the Newman Government, it seemed the lights went out, doors closed and a sense of fear and panic set in.

Any political change naturally brings policy changes with it, reflecting a different set of priorities, and will be accompanied by some level of budget change, which may include reductions. What I, and many others, did not expect was the ill informed, cavalier and at the end of the day unproductive actions that would follow and in particular the repercussions for the arts.

Governments at the extreme ends of the spectrum often act from conviction, without feeling the need to seek advice from the bureaucracy, from industry experts, or from evidence built up over years. The framing policy of the new Queensland Government appeared to be *'it is our turn now'*. Advice seemed to come from a handful of disaffected individuals who felt that they had not been heard under the previous government, and everything that had happened in the past (good and bad) was deemed to be wrong. It seemed to be okay in this context for a single Minister to take decisions on where the $12.4 million of cuts to the arts would fall, without seeking advice or analysis on how to do least harm and achieve the new Government's stated objectives.

So in a portent of what was to come at federal level, the cut was focused on the most vulnerable—the small-to-medium arts sector. The arguments in favour of maintaining the funding for the larger organisations (major performing arts and statutory bodies) were put forward in the context of the economy and 'cultural tourism', the longer planning times required for the larger organisations, and the need to maintain a partnership with the Federal Government for their funding. Yet the Newman Government had been elected as a government for small business, and there were those in the small-to-medium sector who also had federal funding that required them to match it from other sources including the State Government. In a scenario like this it doesn't matter how much evidence you have—convictions and world view are more powerful influences that facts.

At its most basic, this was the only place in Arts Queensland where the Government had any flexibility to make cuts. Preserving federal funds for the small-to-medium sector is not deemed as important (smaller scale of funds, less visible risk) and this sector's work is less known to individual politicians—though collectively they engage with many more people throughout the State than the larger Brisbane-based organisations.

A skewed process will always lead to skewed outcomes. Despite the good will and intentions of many involved (peers, bureaucrats and members of the Government's newly appointed Investment Advisory Board) the process appeared mired in lack of knowledge and experience of both the sector and government processes. Its bureaucracy was fearful—rightly so, with the consequent loss of thousands of jobs throughout the public sector and the high-profile departure of a senior arts bureaucrat. In effect all the experience in the world would not have led the Government to change its direction.

The Government was seemingly unwilling to reason its way to get the best outcome and unprepared to consider any other approach to change. It would have taken only a small amount of money to give those companies losing funding a 12 to 24-month window (as had happened in the past) in which to consider their future and plan for different circumstances. The LNP Government found need for this in other areas: for example in Health it had decided to de-fund 20-plus community health organisations. In this case it guaranteed those organisations two years' funding and put them through a planning and development process to create the changes necessary for them to survive within the new funding arrangements. This was a strategic approach for change using government money wisely to find new solutions, whatever the merits of the initial decision.

Over twenty applicant arts organisations received no funding at all in the 2013 grant round, including a handful of those that had been receiving triennial funding. Their experiences since then have varied. Two did close down and I would say these were already weakened at the time by other factors: loss of clarity of vision and mission, weaknesses in governance and very limited sources of alternative funding. Unfortunately, both these organisations were from the youth arts sector. Other companies that survived were wounded, but at that stage not mortally. Those that were confident of their vision and driven by their passion (a core characteristic of a resilient organisation) rallied their communities, found some project money from other government programs and philanthropic grants; and successfully negotiated some 'bridging' support from Arts Queensland. They were probably those companies that in less extraordinary circumstances would not have lost their funding.

If you passionately believe in what you are doing, as most organisations (and all small businesses) do, you will hang on to see if things will get better. After all, the primary 'client' for the work had been the State Government, purchasing arts and cultural services for communities. There was a belief that this 'market' would pick up again; that a future government would recognise the public value generated by their work. Some of those organisations have since changed their business models but still believe they are unsustainable without securing government support in the future. For example, organisations are dipping into limited financial reserves, have become too reliant on one or two individuals who have taken on extra responsibilities (sometimes at Board level and in a voluntary capacity), and in some cases been driven to sell assets which could with better planning have been used to derive an income stream for the future.

When new money was secured for the arts a year later (thanks to the work of a new Arts Minister and the Investment Advisory Board) the focus was on assisting organisations to build capacity for change, a topic which is explored in more detail later in this paper. It was too late for the organisations which had already lost their funding.

There remains one further issue to address from the decisions in 2013. Those organisations that were funded, some with a small increase, nevertheless found their funding reduced over three years, so that in the next financial year they will be receiving support at the same level they were in 2012/13. The decisions have left a number of small-to-medium arts organisations in a weakened state to face the turmoil now anticipated at a federal level. *'We have been trying for seven years to get out of the poverty cycle—we have no more juice to squeeze'* was how one CEO put it to me.

As well as the repercussions for artists and the professional development of different forms of arts practice in the State, what we really have to question is the poor economics of such decisions; the waste of time and energy expended by all sides; and the disregard for the Government's long-term investment in the cultural and social (if not financial) capital of these organisations. The change is being required by Government and too often the organisations are the ones being made to feel that they are the failures. They are too busy delivering the outputs and outcomes required by existing funding contracts and lack the time and support to make changes they know they need to make for the future. More experienced people will be lost from the sector, more pathways for artists will close, including new generations of graduates from our tertiary system. We await with interest the outcome of the review of arts funding programs currently being undertaken by the new Queensland Government, but with the changes that have occurred at a federal level, the situation for some is very bleak.

On a brighter note, I attended a presentation recently from the CEOs of two non-profit organisations on why they had decided to merge. One was a small-to-medium

Queensland arts organisation BEMAC (originally Brisbane Ethnic Music and Art Centre), the other a significantly larger organisation, a community employment support service, Access Community Services Ltd, which has a focus on improving labour market participation by vulnerable job seekers including newly arrived migrants. Although only in the early stages of the new merged entity, this is an interesting story in which seemingly very different organisations recognised their shared grass roots history, values, cultural, social and economic vision for the future and were prepared to work together for mutual benefit.

> *The Arts is recognised as an important part of the settlement and development journey. It has provided a vehicle for new migrants and refugees to express themselves, their challenges, their dreams and their triumphs. It has also been a platform to celebrate the talents and contributions of our newest Australians, especially our young people.*[13]

It is anticipated that the merger will deliver benefits for both organisations including positioning them as specialists in using arts-led practice approaches in settlement services. But specifically for BEMAC in the short term, the merger will deliver new investment for the next three years enabling an increase in income-generating activities and increased state-wide reach for their services. There is no doubt that a range of more formal partnerships, alliances and in some cases mergers, will form a part of the arts landscape as well as the broader non-profit and private sectors over the next few years. I believe arts organisations should go on the front foot and explore and embrace such opportunities, within and beyond the arts and cultural sector.

4. Let the policy mirror the ecology

> *A specific policy for the arts needs to be placed within a framework that recognises the arts sector as part of the broader cultural sector and creative industries within which the work of artists is valued for its intrinsic and instrumental, cultural, social and economic benefits.*[14]

From the early 1990s in the UK and in some parts of Europe, the subsidised 'arts' had been recognised alongside the creative industries as being part of a broader cultural sector that could play a key role of re-generating many cities as traditional industries declined. This approach was not dissimilar in some ways to how post-war Britain went about investing in cultural infrastructure for the wellbeing of the people and the nation: from the creation of the Festival of Britain site on the south bank of the Thames to the publication of model *Plans for an Arts Centre* for all local councils in 1945 by the Arts Council of Great Britain.[15]

This understanding of the cultural ecology in the early 1990s in part came from an analysis of the labour market, including the training, skills and pathways required for all those who worked across commercially driven (for profit) or public benefit (non-profit) elements of this sector whether as creators, administrators, technicians or educators. It naturally incorporated discussions on how those with a creative arts training also went on to impact on the development of many other industries and sectors of the economy. Hence research incorporated new ideas for the funding and financing of all aspects of this sector from individual artists to large scale commercial producers, including mapping out the focus and role of government agencies and the private sector along the value chain. The significant injections of European funding in regions such as North-West England, Ireland and Southern Italy into cultural development, arts and the creative industries, came not from the Cultural Directorate (focused primarily on issues of tangible heritage) but the Economic Directorate focused on employment.

At the same time the 'arts' lost the lowly status of being an 'Office' in the early 1990s when the Department of National Heritage (DNH) was formed under a Conservative government. This then became the Department of Culture, Media and Sport under Labour in 1997, still a small department in the grand scheme of things but of recognised importance and helped by its role in the distribution of National Lottery Funds, which included the Olympics and Millennium projects. (Design is a joint responsibility of DCMS and the Department for Business, Innovation and Skills.)

I would argue that this 'joined-up thinking' and an integrated Ministry have been of significant benefit to artists and the arts in England over the past two decades, leading to investment in the whole concept of Creative Britain under the Blair Government; the creation of Nesta;[16] significant relationships between flagship institutions such as the BBC and the subsidised arts sector in new writing, and latterly digitisation; and most recently the formation of the Creative Industries Federation. The latter (which will I write about later) has just published a report to explain why top British entrepreneurs and business leaders see public investment in culture as crucial to what they do.[17]

It came as a surprise to me that a similar approach was not taking place in Australia when I settled here in the late 1990s. Australia had in many ways been ahead of the UK and other nations with this thinking, including through the publication of the Federal Government's cultural policy *Creative Nation* in 1994. Instead what I witnessed was a new policy rhetoric around my understanding of what were the 'cultural industries'—one that drove a wedge between those individuals and organisations that required upfront investment in creative development and on-going contracts from government for activities delivering cultural and social value; and the more commercial companies which through mass reproduction or exploitation of intellectual property could generate significant profits.

For me there were fatal flaws in the thinking underpinning this paradigm, which have unfortunately left a mark on how federal and state government policies have developed today.

The first was *not taking the starting point as being the artist or the creative practitioner and understanding the motivations behind an individual's practice*, which will of course vary during the course of a week let alone throughout an entire career! This is what drives the business and financing models for artists and arts organisations: governments are just another class of 'market' players in this economy through their payment for public services.

The second seemed to be *a view that somehow the old modes of creation and distribution (including live performance in front of real people) would die out with the advent of technology*. It gave no recognition to the basic human need to gather with others to celebrate, participate in and comment on the world around us, let alone the desire to purchase a 'unique' work of art rather than a mass-produced artefact. Governments hungry for new industries and new sources of employment growth have tended to seize on these ideas, with the result that the so-called 'subsidised' arts and artists were further marginalised in early iterations of policy. This has benefited neither the arts nor the creative industries, because to date I am unaware of any significant government investment that has been made in the latter.

The third was *an even deeper issue: the complete disconnect in the narrative between the cultural heart and histories of Australia*, and in particular Aboriginal and Torres Strait Islander art and cultures, which have led me in the last decade to so much greater understanding of the importance to human lives of the relationship between culture, art, society and the economy. This foundation, together with the cultural diversity of the nation (the result of successive waves of immigration) creates the stories, the art, the cultural products that truly define what Australia is. They give us our unique identity and are where we engage best with the rest of the world—think Bangarra, Circa, Back to Back, Stalker, Gurrumul, Big hART and the multitude of international visual arts and new media partnerships. This distinctive cultural energy needs to be at the heart of our framing of policy for culture and creativity

I was introduced to the UNESCO framework for cultural statistics[18] by cultural economists Professors David Throsby and Justin O'Connor and with the integration of Aboriginal and Torres Strait Islander Arts, have used it in my work since. This framework, conceived to collect comparable data across international borders, places individual sub-sectors of the cultural economy within a series of related clusters and identifies the place of elements such as training and education, which transcend sectoral 'silos'. Placed together with the concept of a 'culture cycle', unlike a traditional linear value chain, the framework recognises that different forms and stages of cultural activity are interlinked and interdependent, giving structure and form to an ecosystem in which all the elements interact and are mutually dependent.[19]

It is the only framing I have seen which gets anywhere near the mark of what I witness in the cultural sector on a day-to-day basis. I would agree with Professors Julianne Schultz and Justin O'Connor and others who have written on this subject recently, that only with this clear understanding of these relationships can governments find the appropriate policy levers, including where investment is needed in the 'cycle', to enable both our culture and the industries that emerge from it to grow.

> *The cultural sector should be framed as a complex service sector, involving producer, social and personal services as well as links to manufacture and wholesale/retail. It can be compared to health and education as core 'public goods', but it is a more complex, dispersed and fragmented sector with few sectoral bodies to represent it.*[20]

Would a Productivity Commission Inquiry into the entire cultural economy framed in this way help to advance the sophistication of policy analysis and thinking? If so, I would add my voice to those now calling for one. But we would need a government that was going to move back into an evidence based policy environment to take on board any recommendations. And I would also agree that for anything to seriously come of its findings, a Ministry would need to be created at a federal level which brought the disparate areas of this 'economy' together as recently stated by Julianne Shultz:

> *This does not mean that governments control and direct culture [. . .] rather it recognises that if this sector is to achieve its potential for citizens, companies and the national interest, it needs to be taken seriously and that government needs to work on ways to enable a sustainable, innovative and profitable sector.*[21]

Such a Ministry will need to be more than an aggregation of current Commonwealth functions in arts and culture: it will need to have the authority, and the resources, to build policy leadership and thinking in a way which has not yet been realised.

The major performing arts

In fact only by re-framing the sector in this way can we truly begin to see where the major performing arts organisations sit in the grand scheme of things. Some of the best work we see in Australia is as a result of the endeavours of the Major Performing Arts Companies and I know that they (at least the majority) are feeling under siege from the protests they are getting from the rest of the sector at the moment. But the problem is the system which segregates one group of companies from the winds of change that blow hot and cold on everyone else: it's like trying to protect a water supply for wheat farmers without looking at the impact on other crops and on all natural systems. We need a complete re-think of this categorisation, and here are three simple reasons:

Labels

The concept of 'majors' and 'small-to-medium' organisations is a construct of the funding system: one is not subservient to the other; one group doesn't aspire to be the other and the so-called small-to-medium sector relates as much, if not more, to the rest of the cultural and creative sector as it does to the 28 major performing arts organisations. The small-to-medium sector is much more than a 'second tier' to the majors. It is made up of creatively ambitious professional artists, searching for excellence in their unique endeavours, and it is the test bed for new forms and ideas—a source of R&D for the entire cultural economy and for much of the original work in the Australian vernacular that we see. *It is not simply the training ground for the majors, nor is it, as some recent commentary has suggested, limited to community arts, important though that work is.*

Impacts

Perceptions about the cultural contribution and value for money created by the two sectors tend to be skewed in favour of the majors. But they are mistaken. Small-to-medium sector organisations tour more internationally (18% of all tours were undertaken by the majors and 82% by the small-to-medium sector between 2010 and 2014);[22] employ more artists; create more works including new works by Australian artists; and undertake the majority of regional touring.[23] On international audience data alone, Brisbane-based Circa has a higher attendance than all majors put together. It appears that none of this evidence informed the decisions taken by Minister Bates in Queensland or Minister Brandis in Canberra.

Capacity for change

Finally there is the issue of capacity to change and adapt. These organisations have had on-going support for nearly 15 years, have not had to compete for funding, and indeed have attracted additional tranches of funding on repeated occasions from both sides of government. Many have built up their balance sheets, extended their audiences and developed extensive partnerships with the private sector and other organisations. In this changing environment, are they not the organisations most capable of considering different business models and new relationships with governments? And if not, surely we should be asking why?

5. Funding vs Financing

To be sustainable, every individual or organisation requires confidence, which stems from respect and a supportive environment. With confidence comes the ability to take control of one's future.[24]

It was in the UK in the 1990s that I first became interested in exploring new sources of money for the arts. It was clear then that government support coupled with limited amounts of sponsorship was not enough to sustain the needs of the growing number of artists and small scale creative businesses emerging, particularly in urban areas like Liverpool where I was based. Long before ideas such as social investment and impact investing had really taken off I was working on the early stages of European-funded research, including the early stages of the *Banking on Culture* initiative. These introduced me to new ideas of financing for non-profits: local exchange trading schemes, peer-to-peer lending, investment schemes for creative businesses etc. [25]

What excited me from the start about these new models was the sense that the individual artist, arts organisation or community could be enabled to create their own destiny—whatever their purpose and motivation—if they had more control over their financing model. In simple terms what this could mean was the capacity to have more control of the work you wanted to create.

But sadly it is too often the case that when discussion starts about exploring new models of funding for the arts it is played out in the context of government decreasing its support and trying to find alternative sources, rather than increasing and diversifying income streams to reflect the value being enhanced. Which is a shame because I believe that if the outcome is going to be to create more sustainable ways of working for artists, and organisations delivering much more value for the public and the economy in the long term, then it is a sound argument for increased government investment!

One of the first things that struck me on arrival in Australia was the lack of diversity of funding sources available to artists and small scale creative businesses: which is why, in partnership with accountant Brian Tucker, our company Positive Solutions set up the micro loan scheme QuickstART, reported on below. Moving a single pot of money between different programs within a portfolio to be distributed in a new way as the former Arts Minister has done for the proposed National Program for Excellence in the Arts, does not equate to increasing the diversity of funding. Diversity requires a bigger range of government departments or agencies, organisations, and individuals who are willing to invest in or pay for the arts or artistic experiences, opening up opportunities to increase the funding available across the system.

Diversity also does not mean focusing on a single solution for the future of funding and financing the arts—such as grant-based philanthropy, which has been a key focus for Creative Partnerships Australia.[26] Grants, philanthropy, sponsorship, increased earned income, and investment through different forms of debt and equity finance will all play a part in the financial model for an arts organisation of the future. The current emphasis on one-off philanthropic grants directed to individual organisations as the sole solution is problematic for many reasons, including:

- The limited number of larger philanthropic opportunities outside Melbourne and Sydney;
- The one-off grant based nature of most philanthropy with required program outcomes (and often requiring matching funding);
- The debilitating investment in time and energy needed to deliver highly specific results, often tangential to mission;
- The message from philanthropists that they are not there to replace government funding to the arts in Australia; and
- The growing interest from the philanthropic community in strategic approaches to sustainability and capacity building for organisations beyond the traditional one-off program grants.

Evidence is emerging from the UK that there are constraints to what can be achieved in growing philanthropy to the arts within a specific, limited timeframe. Some reports claim that arts organisations have not been able to raise the matching funding for endowments through the Catalyst Program and Arts Council England had abandoned plans for a second stage.[27] This program was part of a £68 million culture sector-wide scheme to help heritage and arts organisations increase support from fundraising activities. Although it has had some success in building the skills and fundraising capacity of arts organisations, some applicants have expressed concern about the time frames, the focus on philanthropic support over sponsorship and earned income; and the lack of time organisations have to focus on business development while reporting on the delivery of arts outcomes.

Grants vs non-restricted income

Some commentators have suggested that the sector itself prefers grants; not just for reasons of familiarity but because of an inadequate understanding of different types of money and how best to meet financial need.

> *The perception is that grants and donations are 'free money'. This ignores the fact that such money is rarely free.*[28]

The term 'non-restricted income' applies to any source of funding or finance that is not directly linked to a set of specific outcomes and can be used to do whatever an organisation (or individual artist) wants. It can be used to invest in a new show, new equipment, new staff member or be put away for a rainy day. The problem with historical funding for the arts has been that we have had very little such income built into our financial models. Grants (both from government and the private sector) are usually based on delivery of program outcomes; this is the case whether or not they are framed as 'operating' grants or project grants, whether they are one off or provided over a three-year time frame. Although governments and other investors sometimes think they are contributing to the development of a stable organisation, they are in reality buying services for their communities.

Grants never cover full costs, so other income sources—including what may be seen as 'un-restricted' income such as box office revenue—go into the delivery of a program only part-funded by a specific grant. While those organisations funded for three years report on their organisational capacity (on top of the impacts of the art they deliver), the money for operating in the small-to-medium sector pays for core staff to oversee the delivery of that art or raise funds to cover program costs, not for strengthening their organisations. And until quite recently, it was seen (by both governments and philanthropists) as 'not the right thing' to make a surplus at the end of a year. This is a complete misunderstanding of the term 'non-profit' as applied to the legal status of an organisation.

The six-year funding dilemma

So, as a result of the historical funding framework, we have, outside the 28 major performing arts organisations, an arts sector in which the majority of players are under-capitalised and ill prepared to make the changes that are required for the future. The six-year program to have been introduced this year by the Australia Council, but now suspended, would have been a game changer for some

170 arts companies and built the stability required in this core group of organisations. The inability to follow through with that program will impact badly on a change process for which many in the sector were already preparing—a process responsive to the new 'zeitgeist' and one which above all others deserved government support.

Six-year funding would have strengthened organisations in so many ways, by:

- *Underpinning the ability to leverage funds from other sources.* There is clear evidence to support this view. I understand that the Key Producers involved in the trial of six-year funding between 2008 and 2013 leveraged this support nearly 8 to 1, so if the Australia Council had invested the $30 million planned in the small-to-medium sector, it would have multiplied to $240 million per year (or $1.4 billion over six years) in other funding and financing for arts activity across the country.[29]
- *Enabling them to build their audiences, networks, connectivity* and deepen engagement with communities creating more long-term and meaningful impacts, which was so evident from impact on those Key Producer organisations.
- *Achieving investment in the right staff* to develop both the art and enterprise aspects of their work.
- *Helping organisations to strengthen their balance sheets* and gain some working capital from which to invest in new work and enterprise initiatives, including exploring new forms of financing.

From a sector perspective it would have created a national infrastructure of organisations from which to build, and assist smaller project-based companies, individual artists, local government and regional arts initiatives. It would have delivered more value for money for the government—surely something that must reflect broader current government policy. Instead, if the new National Program for Excellence in the Arts goes ahead, the money that would have supported building resilient organisations will be used to keep them compliant and mendicant through the out-of-date, one-off grant process.

The changing face of philanthropy

Like the Australia Council, which based its new funding framework on extensive research and evidence of need, some in the philanthropic community are beginning to take a more strategic approach to change and investment; working in partnership with each other and with government agencies to deliver better outcomes for artists and communities. But they too need to know they can continue to work with the sector and with governments and that the goal posts won't keep changing.

Examples of such projects include:

- A new capacity-building stream from the Myer Foundation, at this stage a pilot program for organisations in Victoria or Tasmania which will be assessed partly on the recipient's capacity to increase in connectivity, one of key characteristics of resilience.
- The inaugural IMPACT Philanthropy

Partnership program from investment and trustee group Perpetual. This has just been announced and will distribute $6.2million to eight not-for-profit organisations including one arts organisation Big hART with over $700,000 for a five-year capacity-building program to commercialise productions.

- The partnership between the Tim Fairfax Family Foundation and the Queensland Government to create the Arts Business Innovation Fund (ABIF) which is described in more detail below.

Many philanthropists are viewing with interest moves by Foundations in the US to use all their assets towards their mission; using grants and loans for capacity-building and becoming actively engaged in impact investing, including rating companies for such factors as their social and environmental impact.

Which leads to the issue of impact investing and where this fits in the future schema of arts funding. Coupled with the issue of strengthening organisations through building non-restricted income streams is the introduction of debt and equity financing into the funding equation for the arts, using the growth of impact investing to *increase*, not replace the sources organisations and individuals have at their disposal. Impact investing can best be described as:

> *Investments made into companies, organisations or specialised funds with the intention to generate social, environmental and cultural impacts alongside a financial return.*[30]

There are many different models, structures and players in this emerging field but for non-profit organisations the most common products have been focused on debt financing because of the prohibition on distribution of profits. The inclusion of 'financing' as well as funding for 'non-profits' has been accepted in the US and UK for more than a decade. Here I'm going to focus on examples from the UK, which make a useful comparison with Australia because public expectation and understanding of the role of government in funding the arts has been similar to ours.

Live Theatre in Newcastle is one leading performing arts organisation focusing on new writing that has used loan financing on top of government grants and philanthropy. It has built an asset base including a pub and commercial offices as well as a range of enterprises generating income from its creative work. A recent report for Arts Council England and the Theatre Development Trust has recommended that ACE also explore the use of loans and return on investment schemes as a suite of measures to support the development of touring in the UK.[31]

Creative England is an offshoot of the Arts Council of England and was established as an independent Community Interest Company (CIC) to carry on the work of Creative Industry Finance.[32] It also manages *Own Art* and *Take it Away,* loan finance for purchasers of art which have been used as models for the development of *Collect Art* in Tasmania and *Art Money* in Sydney. Creative England's purpose is to provide a range of financial products and services designed to enable the growth and development of the UK's cultural and creative industries. It is creating a network of lenders including some interested in social enterprise, some micro finance and some larger lenders and exploring their own fund for arts organisations based on a 'convertible loan' structure where the loan could be repaid or converted to equity in the company.

Then there is the recently launched Arts Impact Fund (AIF) which has been in development for the last couple of years following moves by an independent group of arts professionals to create new sources of funding and finance. It is a £7 million investment fund that will provide unsecured loan finance to arts organisations (and museums) that demonstrate excellence in their artistic practice and social impact.

The AIF has been created with the help of the UK Cabinet Office, which is exploring new opportunities for the co-mingling of funds, and involves a group of investors: Bank of America Merrill Lynch, Esmée Fairbairn Foundation and Nesta[33] supported by ACE with additional funding from the Calouste Gulbenkian Foundation. The fund is being seen as a demonstration project to show how the co-mingling of funds from different agencies can work: how 'social finance' or impact investing can be used in the context of the arts and how to report the specific outcomes required.

The AIF opened in April 2015 for unsecured loans ranging from £150,000 to £600,000, with an interest rate of between 4% and 7%. It is anticipated that there will be two rounds per year and the performance of those receiving funds will be measured. Applications are anticipated from those organisations wishing to undertake:

- *Capital development*
- *Cash flow expenditure for a particular initiative*
- *Creation of new products/technologies for distribution*
- *The commercial transfer of productions (in some cases)*

Those who apply will have to show why they need the money and explain the social impact that the investment will make in any of three contexts: youth and educational attainment; community and citizens; and health and wellbeing. They will of course also have to demonstrate how they will repay the loan. Successful applicants will be announced every six months over a two-year period and their performance and impact measurements will be published.

An outstanding example of impact investing in Australia has of course, been by one of our major performing arts organisations: the Australian Chamber Orchestra's Instrument Fund, an unlisted Australian unit trust enabling investors to purchase fine stringed instruments for use by the musicians.[34] But what has been most interesting is that it has principally been organisations in the small-to-medium sector and independent artists that are having to pioneer the use of loans for business and property development through social enterprise development and investment funds (SEDIF) managed through three community finance providers, Foresters Community Finance, Social Ventures Australia and Social Enterprise Finance Australia.

Individual artists are also accessing micro loans for

everything from short term cashflow management to investment in marketing and professional development. QuickstART, now managed on our behalf by Foresters Community Finance,[36] has delivered a mix of no-interest and interest-bearing loans valued at over $150,000 to 44 artists in the last two years. The model has now been copied for two new loan schemes in South Australia, one led by Carclew Youth Arts and the other by Guildhouse.[37]

Yet it is the larger organisations that are the more likely to have the capacity to explore these new avenues of support. I was amazed to be told by one senior arts administrator that ideas for new models are okay for the small-to-medium sector but not for the larger organisations! There is a contradiction here. Of course most of the larger organisations are under less pressure to adapt because of their strong connections to government and the business and philanthropic community. Why go looking for an affordable loan for your new building when it is likely the Government will fund it for you anyway?

Although short-lived, the Investment Advisory Board for the arts in Queensland recognised that new approaches were needed to assist the sector including partnerships to bring new money to the table. The creation of the Arts Business Innovation Fund (ABIF), where half a million dollars in government grant funds has been matched with half a million from the Tim Fairfax Family Foundation. It offers organisations up to $100,000 in matching funding through a mix of a grant and a loan. It is a requirement of the scheme that these funds be specifically directed towards new business development initiatives and to grow future sources of income for companies. The introduction of a small loan component is unique in two ways. Firstly it has come from the corpus of the Fairfax Foundation and therefore does not impact on the grants that the Foundation will also distribute. Secondly it will give arts organisations their first experience of managing a loan as part of their broader financial model in a context which will strengthen their overall long-term financial position.

A word of caution

These initiatives are not a replacement for government funding for the arts but a new form of financing which, applied appropriately, could introduce more dollars into the sector and help strengthen it at the same time. But for me the application of impact investing in the arts must go beyond using the instrumental argument for value (those arts initiatives that have as their core purpose the intent to achieve specific social outcomes, for example in the area of homelessness or health). It is necessary to uphold the fact that cultural engagement and expression in itself play a role in a civil society and community well-being as Robyn Archer so clearly stated in her 2005 Platform Paper:

> *Contact with art can sometimes have an effect that results in change or challenge. It's not necessarily always art with a message that does this. Contact with sheer beauty can often do it. It may well send a strongly affected audience member careering off the path of so-called mainstream values on a hunt for the individual self.*[38]

In any discussion around the application of new models I will contest that arts organisations are 'cultural' not 'social' enterprises delivering first and foremost on a cultural (artistic) mission with added social and economic benefits on the way—in fact the best possible outcomes for all investors. My interest in learning from what is happening in the broader social sector is to help shape and expand new financial products and opportunities for the arts, but the core value must still reside in the value and benefits for society generated by cultural and creative practice. It remains to be seen how the UK Arts Impact Fund described above will determine the criteria for 'well-being' and incorporate a real understanding of cultural as well as social value.

It is also in this space that some of the most interesting conversations are taking place around how both public value and economic development can be captured in a new paradigm for funding and financing and where government, the community and other institutions can work hand in hand to deliver public value and solve some the big societal problems of today. One such initiative is that of Wilson Asset Management in creating a listed investment company that also supports charities. The recently launched Future Generation Global Company, Australia's first listed investment company that is internationally focused, will provide shareholders with exposure to global funds, deliver a market return and donate 1% of net tangible assets a year—a figure of several million dollars—to a named number of charities working with young people with a mental illness. Imagine this for the arts.

Impact investing is providing a significant and growing source of finance which could be more available to the arts sector if introduced in an appropriate and timely way.

6. Stand up and be counted (in more ways than one)

> *The very nature of such 'transformational' impacts needs longitudinal studies beyond political cycles and the limits of government-funding programs [...] this is not just the responsibility of governments. The arts sector itself must take responsibility for informing the industry generally and the public funding agencies.*[39]

It is clear from the responses to the Senate Inquiry that there is significant evidence available of the volume and impact of the work generated by the small-to-medium sector. Why after all this time of providing information to funding agencies did the Ministers in Queensland and federally have seemingly no interest or knowledge of this? The reasons appear to be diverse and complex. Funding for each of the major organisations is the subject of a set of formal agreements between the two tiers of government, so that Ministers in both tiers have little choice but to pay attention to their needs and performance. Because of scale, and because of the nature of audiences, parliamentarians are inclined to make time for the majors' events, and often have business, social and political connections to people serving on their boards. On the other hand, competition for ministerial attention from the four hundred-odd small-to-medium organisations is fierce, and their claims are contesting a huge range of community events of similar scale. More importantly, funding for the small-to-medium sector is not 'ring-fenced' in any structural arrangement, but sits within the relevant agency budget. At federal level, funding for this sector and the relationships are all managed through the Australia Council, so that federal bureaucrats have no direct knowledge of the work of this sector per se, and no need to collect data or analyse or report on its contribution.

Perhaps the job of collating information about the sector has been left for too long to the funding agencies and universities, including the Australia Council through its research and advocacy role. But what is the use, if at times like this the Australia Council is unable to advocate and only provides the facts relating to the impact of the decision after the event, as it has done so usefully in its submission to the Senate Inquiry? It seems that in this environment and as currently constituted, the Australia Council is unable to fulfil the role as advocate for the arts without being seen to be somehow feathering its own nest, despite it having in its authorising legislation, responsibilities for both advocacy for the arts, and for providing formal advice to the Federal Government. Why this is so difficult for the Australia Council is a mystery. Does Government argue that the Australian Research Council (ARC) or the National Health and Medical Research Council (NH&MRC) are acting out of self-interest when they report on the state of scientific or medical research, the performance of the Australian research sector, or the need for additional funding to keep pace with international trends?

The sector also needs to work collectively for the future of the arts; and stand together against poor policy making that has a profound impact on the well-being of any part of the ecosystem. If not, why would anyone else stand up for the arts in the future? We need to applaud the work that those in the sector have done around the #freethearts campaign and the voluntary alliance for the sector ArtsPeak which has ensured that the real facts about the impact of the sector are coming to light.[40] We need to be reminded of Wesley Enoch's Platform Paper written only twelve months ago which lamented the state of cultural leadership—admitting that he made a mistake in not saying more at the time of the Queensland Government cuts. We need to think seriously about what happens next.

Which takes me back to the newly formed Creative Industries Federation in the UK—here is one model, formed by leaders across the arts and creative industries (subsidised and commercial) in recognition of the same failure of advocacy and messaging:

> *It is time for the UK's creative community to take control of its own destiny. There is an urgent need for the sector to speak with a strong, independent voice, bringing together the UK's public arts, creative industries and cultural education. Through our lobbying, research and networks we will increase the impact of a sector that, lacking a unified independent voice, has sometimes failed to pack a political punch*

that matches its social and economic contribution. [41]

If we want this to happen effectively in Australia, we will need to develop an approach which is collaborative and sophisticated; is broadly representative of the entire cultural sector and economy; and is funded and financed by its members and supporters.

Besides a strong and united sector voice, we also need an independent source of policy, research and thinking. For example, a policy institute for the cultural sector and economy, like the Grattan Institute,[42] or simply a stream within that Institute. The current campaign must go beyond redressing the present crisis: it must be about changing the environment that led to the decisions in the first place, and influencing it and public thinking into the future. Politicians respond to public opinion, and the true task here is to create an informed and critical public, with a good understanding of the cultural sector and economy and its many contributions. Appropriate political decision-making will follow.

There are many areas of research such an Institute could pursue:

- Researching the significant changes happening internationally in the area of paying for public value, its funding and its measurement; and determining how this impacts on the arts and cultural economy;

- Working with other sectors to promote the broader emerging concepts of value measurement beyond GDP, including the new international integrated accounting framework; and

- Exploring the idea and benefit of new forms of legal entity and how these might benefit the arts sector. Perhaps an Institute could also ensure adequate support was provided to the Australian Bureau of Statistics (ABS) to capture the statistical data required to provide an evidence base for policy and decision making.

Of course, we also need an arts sector that collects and reports on the impact it creates in a way that is appropriate to its own objectives—the stories as well as the statistics—and to encourage any future investment into individual organisations and the sector. But we also need a respected independent voice to analyse this information and present it in the broader context of public policy making for the future, assisting the Australia Council and ministries at state and federal level.

7. Changing the paradigm: The Money Story

If we truly want our artists to succeed and to be recognised at home and overseas for their *excellence* and if we want our citizens actively engaged in arts and cultural activities in building strong healthy communities, then we need resilient organisations and a stable environment from which to create, experiment and grow. It is of course important that governments implement the policy platform on which they were elected. But is it also not the responsibility of governments to balance their desire for change with their responsibility for stewardship: to do no harm, particularly in times of immense social and technological upheaval?

I believe the funding decisions by the former federal Arts Minister have not been in the best interest of effectiveness and efficiency (one of the key reasons for moving a group of federal government funding programs to the Australia Council in 2013) and not in the best interest of building resilient organisations. Nor have they been in the best interest of government policy for long term *jobs and growth*, nor in the best interest of the public, who want to engage with the arts in many ways, well beyond the mainstream of the 28 major performing arts organisations. I also believe that the nature of the ministerial decision-making we have seen, including relying on incomplete figures and information, goes against the fundamental principles of good government and accountability, which we need to be able to have trust in the systems which underpin our society.

Throughout this paper I've made a number proposals for the future—encouraged arts organisations to think outside the box in relation to mergers and alliances; proposed consideration of both a new representative arts sector body and a broader cultural-sector policy think tank to strengthen the voice and general understanding of the role of the arts and all aspects of cultural engagement in Australia today.

I will conclude with some specific ideas about the structures and systems we need for funding and financing of the arts into the future. Australia is not the only country grappling with these issues.

While I was writing this paper, the UK Government announced its intention to set out a vision and agenda for the future of the arts, culture and heritage sector; and has commenced a series of online, open discussions to inform the paper. It will be the first overview of the Government's role in supporting these cultural sectors since Jennie Lee, the first Minister for the Arts, published the very first White Paper on the arts 50 years ago. It will explore four key themes:

- *place: the role that culture plays in creating places that people want to live, work and visit;*
- *people: and how they engage with culture;*
- *culture: as a tool for promoting Britain abroad; and*

- *the funding models and how they can contribute to financial resilience in the sector.*

In Australia, do we need a complete re-think or can some fundamental changes be made to the basic framework we have, to strengthen the system for the future?

The Australia Council

The 2000-plus submissions to the Senate Inquiry have been made because there are some longstanding principles at stake. And not just principles for the arts. Nobody wants a society where only the people with direct access to politicians exercise influence over the use of public money, and over the lives of others.

Do we want a system, and a body within that system. that upholds a 'collective and expert' authority around arts investment? And, if we do, is that the Australia Council in its current or an enhanced form? Do we want a body that relies on a peer funding process, has a national sectoral overview, and undertakes sector development initiatives as well as grant delivery? Or is a sector ecology not a real construct and should the make up of the sector be subject to the whims of individuals to be modified at will every time there is a change of federal government? Are we now at a time when it will be every organisation for itself and government only responds to the parts rather than the whole?

2017 will be the fifty-year anniversary of the Australia Council. What are we going to do to ensure that what we value about the Australia Council is preserved into the future, and indeed, that whatever form it takes, the new body has the legal and political authority to do its job effectively? I don't believe we need a review of the Australia Council and what it does. That has been done, a new governance model established and a new strategic plan developed based on extensive consultation with the sector and endorsed by the sitting government, and it was on the verge of being implemented. The Council's need for additional investment to undertake the work required was clearly articulated through that process.

But we may need a very different type of organisation from the one that is currently legislated for—one that can:

- Plan effectively for the future and for its entire budget and operations, without fear of unilateral intervention from the responsible Minister;
- Rely on diverse sources of financial input, so that it itself is less vulnerable to change, through partnerships with the private sector and the development of new investment mechanisms;
- Provide a range of different investment opportunities for the sector beyond grants, working with other finance providers to create specific products of benefit to artists and arts organisations;
- Invest in the long-term resilience of artists and arts organisations without always requiring direct immediate program outcomes in return;
- Work with a new industry body and policy institute on research which will report on the impacts of the sector, provide the best possible advice to government on how best to invest in

the sector and provide the best value for money;
- Be at the forefront of reporting its achievements through an integrated financial reporting mechanism which can measure all aspects of cultural, social and economic value from its investments to all partners.

The present Australia Council Act enables the Council to do much of what is outlined here: receive funds from non-government sources, develop and implement different approaches to investment (including making loans), partner and collaborate with other bodies, and develop enhanced reporting mechanisms (provided it meets the formal requirements for Australian Government-owned entities).

What is needed, however, is clear support from the Australian Government for it to use these powers much more extensively than it has done in the past.

For this to happen, the Minister of the day and the Board of the Australia Council need to jointly develop an agenda for realising these changes, which should then be formalised in both the Minister's instructions to the Council each year, and in the targets for achievement laid out in the Council's strategic plan, and updated annually.

Investment Fund

A more significant change would relate to management of a new investment fund under the Council's purview—that is, a source of non-government revenue to ensure a better level of stability in arts funding and long-term planning. A new investment arm of the Council could be set up, rather like the foundations which many major publicly-owned arts bodies already operate, to manage its funds attraction and investment process. Some thought has gone into how such a fund would operate as a result of the consultation undertaken for the concept of a Foundation for the Artist through the *New Models New Money* initiative funded by the Centre for Social Impact (CSI) and Arts Queensland between 2009 and 2011.[43]

Obviously, whether this would need to be a separate body or could operate within the legal entity of the Council would require legal advice. The Canada Council for the Arts was originally established with an endowment as well as receiving government funds annually, which grows each year from investments but also from new donated funds from individuals, corporations, and foundations. Senior philanthropists and investment advisors would need to lead such a project, and at least two of the members should be represented on the Council's Board.

A body of this kind which is able to bring significant funds to the table, and manage them in the long term interest of the nation's cultural endeavour, will significantly change the standing of the Council—'from leaners to lifters', to quote a recent federal Treasurer.

Whereas I believe that philanthropic dollars should go to adding value and not correcting errors of government, I also believe the time is right for those contributing through their own foundations to work more closely with the Australia Council to play a more *strategic role* in the development of the arts in Australia and ensure government maintains its on-going support as the principle investor. This goes well beyond the remit of Creative Partnerships Australia, whose role is to work with *the sector itself* on developing its capacity to attract non-government support.

A Cultural Ministry

As for a future Cultural Ministry and the role of that Ministry in direct grants making, I believe such a Minister should have a grant program but not one that mirrors the work of the Australia Council by aiming to support excellence in the professional arts sector, as has just been created. What is needed within any new Cultural Ministry is a brief which complements the work of the Australia Council. Such a program would address the other side of the cultural equation: how citizens access and experience arts and culture. A national program of this kind would support touring by regional as well as metropolitan companies, and by cultural heritage organisations, including museums and libraries. It would also support the development and presentation of work reflecting Australia's cultural diversity; and maintain regional arts and cultural physical infrastructure (in partnership with state and local governments). This—ensuring access to publicly funded opportunities—is mainstream work for government departments, and enables issues such as a geographic, social and cultural spread of public funding to be taken into account.

Managing the range of companies

And what of the current notion of dividing the arts sector into the major performing arts and the small-to-medium sector? I want to suggest an alternative approach.

Let the sector determine which are the national companies—five to seven at most. The choice could vary from time to time and ideally would include a national theatre based on the ideas emerging from the National Indigenous Theatre Forum and the discussions created by Julian Meyrick on the idea of a National Theatre Workshop.[44] The national companies should be funded by the Federal Government, and should be subject to six-yearly reviews to determine their on-going entitlement to inclusion in this group. This process and the ensuing contracts and evaluation would be managed by the Australia Council, and include *international* as well as national peers in the evaluation process.

All other companies (including those currently identified as 'major') should then be considered as key organisations within their state and art form and compete for federal funding (preferably in a re-introduced six-year cycle) through the Australia Council, and through their state/territory governments—as part of a *national portfolio* of organisations. And let's call them such and remove the language of majors and small-to-medium companies but at the same time ensure more formal agreements between the federal and state governments for this portfolio. At this stage some of the existing major and medium scale companies might wish to take the road suggested by Katharine Brisbane in Platform Paper no 43[45] and create more commercial vehicles for some of their work utilising the growth of impact investing.

Growing the total pool of resources

For too long it has been individual arts organisations that have been asked to change their funding and financing models without focusing on the need to change the overall systems of financing for the sector. It's the turn of governments and other interested investors to share this burden utilising some of their resources to create a strong and resilient sector and grow the resources available at a system level to make this happen, beyond one-off project grants to individual organisations. There are signs that new models are out there and are applicable to the arts but more focused thinking and investment are required to bring this about. We are already seeing signs of innovation from the philanthropic community and state governments. It would be good to see the same from the Federal Government.

As I stated in the introduction, Australia does not have an alternative source of support for the arts, one which is managed strategically as in the UK or Canada. Despite the significant cuts made to the arts budget by the UK Government, it is reported that the Arts Council of England 2014/15 budget showed that *a £6.6 million fall in its 'unrestricted' grant-in-aid funding from Government was more than compensated for by a £21.7 million rise in Lottery revenues, plus a further one-off £20.7 million—its share of the proceeds from the sale of the Olympic Park.* The recent focus here on organisation-level initiatives such as one-off matched funding schemes run through Creative Partnerships will not suffice if we want to see sector-wide change.

In our 2008 Platform Paper we added our voice to the need for more investment to build sustainability by proposing a 'Future Fund' for the arts.[46] Looking at how well the Australian Government's existing Future Fund has done over the last eight years growing from an initial investment of $60.5 billion to $110 billion imagine what extra resources a $100 million fund established then for the arts would be generating today?[47]

Numerous ideas for increasing support to the sector through changes in the taxation system have also been mooted, through submissions to the Henry Review of taxation and previous Platform Papers such as the proposals by David Pledger in Platform Paper no 34;[48] and most recently through responses to the Senate Inquiry. These are all worthy of consideration and cover everything from additional direct taxes to more tax incentives for those donating to or participating in arts activities. And as already mentioned we could explore models similar to the Future Generation Global Company which could donate profits back to a specific new change initiative.

There is no shortage of ideas and opportunities to provide for the future long-term health of the sector, but all will require governments and philanthropists to think differently about how they can work together to focus on building the long-term stability and resilience we so badly need.

And finally

Given the speed of change in federal politics today, it could well be that by the time this paper is published, the Senate Committee will have reported, the new Arts Minister will have implemented its suggestions and all will seem well with the world.

However good that might be in the short term, it will still fall short of addressing the big underlying challenges which our cultural sector broadly, and our arts funding systems in particular, face into the future—challenges which are shaped by global conditions and influences every bit as much as they are by one-off local decisions.

So what are the conditions required to enable that vision for a 'culturally ambitious nation' to be fulfilled? There are three core ideas for any federal government action that I want to reiterate here:

- Take a whole view of the broad cultural economy as expressed in the UNESCO framework. Stop treating the arts as a marginal venture. Establish a cultural ministry, which will, as one of its first steps, contribute to a Productivity Commission inquiry into the scale, contribution, and support systems required to facilitate that economy.
- Adopt contemporary funding and financing practices where collaboration is key. Bring together some of the best financial minds in the country to develop some concrete proposals along the lines proposed in this paper, from new forms of taxation to developing a significant endowment or 'Future Fund' for the arts.
- Build the Australia Council into a body which can truly invest in and develop a 'culturally ambitious nation' in partnership with the states and territories and the growing philanthropic sector in Australia; with access to diversified streams of funding as with Arts Council England and the Canada Council for the Arts. Fund for resilience not for dependency.

Let the actions of the last few months be a wake-up call to all concerned with the future of Australian arts and culture.

Endnotes

1 Cathy Hunt and Phyllida Shaw, *A Sustainable Arts Sector: What will it take?* Platform Papers 15. Sydney: Currency House 2008.

2 This figure is taken from the Australia Council for the Arts submission to the Senate Inquiry into the impact of the 2014 and 2015 Commonwealth Budget decisions on the Arts, and includes $105 million for the establishment of a National Program for Excellence in the Arts (NPEA), $6 million for Book Councils, and $7.3 million in efficiency cuts.

3 Leigh Tabrett, *It's Culture, Stupid: Reflections of an arts bureaucrat.* Platform Papers 34. Sydney: Currency House 2013, p.3.

4 *A Culturally Ambitious Nation* is the title of the Australia Council for the Arts Strategic Plan 2014-2019 (http://www.australiacouncil.gov.au/workspace/uploads/strategic-plan.pdf)

5 Lindy Hume. 'Does size matter?' *ArtsHub*, 7 July 2015. http://www.artshub.com.au/news-article/artshub-conference/public-policy/lindy-hume/does-size-matter-248635

6 Liz Hill, 'DCMS told to model for cuts of up to 40%', *Arts Professional*, 22 July 2015. http://www.artsprofessional.co.uk/news/dcms-told-model-cuts-40

7 Andrew Clark, 'Chris Bowen promises a new Labor', *Australian Financial Review*, 10 January 2015. http://www.afr.com/news/politics/national/chris-bowen-promises-a-new-labor-20150109-12lem0

8 B Corporation definition: A benefit corporation (known as a B Corporation) is a for-profit, non-tax exempt entity that is legally able to emphasise its stated social or environmental goals ahead of maximising profits for shareholders. Community interest company definition: A community interest company (CIC) is a new type of company introduced by the United Kingdom government in 2005 under the Companies (Audit, Investigations and Community Enterprise) Act 2004, designed for social enterprises that want to use their profits and assets for the public good.

9 Impact investing definition: Investments made into companies, organisations or specialised funds with the intention to generate social, environmental and cultural impacts alongside a financial return. See Rosemary Addis, John McLeod, Alan Raine, *Impact Australia: Investment for Social and Economic Benefit,* Canberra: Department of Education, Employment and Workplace Relations and JBWere, p.2.

10 See in particular speeches by Robyn Archer including *Science, Society Resilience and the Arts* presented at the ANU in Canberra 18 February 2010; and the work of Mark Robinson in the UK, including his report *Making Adaptive Resilience Real,* Arts Council England, July 2010. http://www.artscouncil.org.uk/media/uploads/making_adaptive_resilience_real.pdf

11 Militant was officially the Revolutionary Socialist League, an element of the UK Labour Party at the time based around the newspaper of the same name formed in 1964. For the story of the Militant Council in Liverpool between 1983 and 1987, see Diane Frost and Peter North, *Militant Liverpool: A City on the Edge,* Liverpool University Press, 2013.

12 Deputy Premier and Treasurer in the Liberal National Coalition Government 1996-98.
13 Gail Ker OAM, CEO Access Community Services. BoardConnect workshop *Alliances and Collaborations,* 15 July 2015, Brisbane.
14 Cathy Hunt and Phyllida Shaw, *A Sustainable Arts Sector: What will it take?* Platform Papers 15, Sydney: Currency House 2008, p.43.
15 *Plans for an Arts Centre.* London, Arts Council of Great Britain 1945.
16 Formerly National Endowment for Science, Technology and the Arts (NESTA).
17 Professor Jonothan Neelands, Eliza Easton, Te-Anne Robles, *How public investment in arts contributes to growth in the creative industries,* UK: Creative Industries Federation 2015.
18 *http://www.uis.unesco.org/culture/Pages/framework-cultural-statistics.aspx*
19 Cathy Hunt, David Fishel, Justin O'Connor, *Gold Coast Cultural Resources Audit Report,* Brisbane, 2012.
20 Justin O'Connor and Mark Gibson, *Culture, Creativity, Cultural Economy: A Review,* ACOLA, 2015. p. 71.
21 Julianne Schultz. 'Cultural economy and the soft power of the forgotten portfolio'. *The Mandarin,* 1 June 2015. http://www.themandarin.com.au/35492-julianne-schultz-culture-arts-economy/
22 Ben Eltham and Joely Mitchell. 'Big companies tour more, do they? George bungles the arts again'. *Crikey,* 20 August 2015. http://www.crikey.com.au/2015/08/20big-companies-tour-more-do-they-george-bungles-the-arts-again/
23 Ben Eltham and Deb Verhoeven, 'Philosophy vs evidence is no way to orchestrate cultural policy', *The Conversation,* 29 May 2015. https://theconversation.com/philosophy-vs-evidence-is-no-way-to-orchestrate-cultural-policy-42487
24 Cathy Hunt and Phyllida Shaw, *A Sustainable Arts Sector: What will it take?* Platform Papers 15. Sydney: Currency House, p.54.
25 Keith Hackett, Peter Ramsden, Danyal Sattar, Christophe Guene, *Banking on Culture: New financial instruments for expanding the cultural sector in Europe,* UK: Banking on Culture Project, Final report, September 2000.
26 www.creativepartnershipsaustralia.org.au. Creative Partnerships Australia facilitates business partnerships, social investment and philanthropy for the cultural and creative sectors.
27 Liz Hill. *Catalyst Endowment loses momentum. Arts Professional,* 11 September 2015. http://www.artsprofessional.co.uk/news/catalyst-endowment-loses-momentum.
28 Emilie Goodall and John Kingston, *Access to Capital—a briefing paper.* UK: Venturesome, 2009. Published in: Margaret Bolton and Clare Cooper. *Capital Matters: How to build financial resilience in the UK's arts and cultural sector,* UK: Mission Models Money, 2011, p.27.
29 Federal Arts submission to the Senate Inquiry into the impact of the 2014 and 2015 Commonwealth Budget decisions on the Arts.
30 Rosemary Addis, John McLeod, Alan Raine, *Impact Australia: Investment for Social and Economic Benefit,* Canberra: Department of Education, Employment and Workplace Relations and JBWere, 2013, p.2.
31 Graham Devlin, Alan Dix. *Theatre Touring in the 21st Century: An exploration of new financial models,* Arts Council England and Theatre Development Trust. UK, 2015.
32 Creative Industry Finance is a program designed to assist creative enterprises and arts cultural organisations in securing the finance and investment needed to develop and grow into sustainable businesses, and is delivered and managed by Creative United. The program was launched across England in September 2014.

33 Formerly National Endowment for Science, Technology and the Arts (NESTA).
34 ACO Instrument Fund: https://www.aco.com.au/support/instrument_fund
35 www.foresters.org.au
36 www.guildhouse.org.au . Originally the craft association of South Australia
37 Robyn Archer, *The Myth of the Mainstream: Politics and the performing arts in Australia today.* Sydney: Currency House Platform Papers no.4, 2005 p.4.
38 Cathy Hunt and Phyllida Shaw, *A Sustainable Arts Sector: What will it take?* Platform Papers 15, Sydney: Currency House, p.45.
39 #freethearts was the hashtag created by ArtsPeak (an unincorporated federation of national peak arts organisations) to galvanise the sector around the idea of a senate inquiry in response to the cuts imposed by Minister Brandis
40 See Creative Industries Federation, http://www.creativeindustriesfederation.com/about/
41 Formed in 2008 through an endowment from the Federal and Victorian Governments, the Grattan Institute is an independent think-tank dedicated to developing high quality public policy in Australia.
42 *New Models New Money, a Foundation for the Artist.* Brisbane: Arts Queensland 2010, http://www.arts.qld.gov.au/docs/full-discussion-paper.pdf
43 Katharine Brisbane, *The Arts and the Common Good*, Platform Papers 43, Sydney: Currency House 2015, p.54.
44 Julian Meyrick, *The Retreat of Our National Drama*, Platform Paper 39, Sydney: Currency House, 2014.
45 Cathy Hunt and Phyllida Shaw, *A Sustainable Arts Sector: What will it take?* Platform Papers 15, Sydney: Currency House, p.54.
46 'Costello has last laugh on Future shock *Australian Business Review*, 28 February 2015. http://www.theaustralian.com.au/business/peter-costello-has-last-laugh-on-future-fund-shock/story-e6frg8zx-1227242195677
47 David Pledger, *Re-valuing the Artist in the New World Order.* Platform Paper 36, Sydney: Currency House, 2013.

Copyright Information

PLATFORM PAPERS
Quarterly essays from Currency House Inc.
Founding Editor: Dr John Golder
Currency House Inc. is a non-profit association and resource centre advocating the role of the performing arts in public life by research, debate and publication.

Postal address: PO Box 2270, Strawberry Hills, NSW 2012, Australia
Email: info@currencyhouse.org.au Tel: (02) 9319 4953
Website: www.currencyhouse.org.au Fax: (02) 9319 3649

ISBN 978 0 9924890 6-9
ISSN 1449-583X

Typeset in Garamond
Printed by Lightning Source
Production by XOU Creative

FORTHCOMING

PP No.46, February 2016
THE DESIGNER: DECORATOR OR DRAMATURG?
Stephen Curtis

The stage designer's role within a performance company is both within and without the company, writes the designer Stephen Curtis, author of *Staging Ideas (*Sydney: Currency Press 2013), the definitive guide to Australian stage and screen design. The designer is a unique observer of the work in creation and a welcome problem solver, the possessor of the 'design solution' when things don't go as planned. The designer's collaborative role could be a model to others, writes Curtis: the role is fluid within the industry and introduces a new kind of creative collaboration. His own working life has been continuously multi-tasking, working concurrently with several directors and creative teams, making work within very different companies/structures/sectors, crossing styles and genres, art forms and media—film, theatre, exhibitions and teaching. It creates a unique 'outsider' position and in turn a unique perspective.

Curtis chooses three productions to give a picture of his work methods including the much acclaimed *The Secret River* (play by Andrew Bovell based on the novel by Kate Grenville), and concludes that today designers are redefining their role and reshaping their careers through specialisation and focus on form over content as a way of exploring and understanding the work they interpret.

Printed in Australia
AUOC01n1221051015
270711AU00008B/22/P

9 780992 489069